W9-CMF-009

The Story of Science

The
Origins
of Life

by Roy A. Gallant

BENCHMARK BOOKS

MARSHALL CAVENDISH
NEW YORK

Series Editor: Roy A. Gallant

Series Consultants:

LIFE SCIENCES
Dr. Edward J. Kormondy
Chancellor and Professor of Biology (retired)
University of Hawaii—Hilo/West Oahu

PHYSICAL SCIENCES
Dr. Jerry LaSala
Department of Physics
University of Southern Maine

Benchmark Books
Marshall Cavendish Corporation
99 White Plains Road
Tarrytown, NY 10591-9001

Library of Congress Cataloging-in-Publication Data
Gallant, Roy A.
        The origins of life / by Roy A. Gallant.
        p. cm. — (Story of science)
Includes bibliographical references (p.).
Summary: Explores the many different myths, theories, and experiments which explain the origin of life, including spontaneous generation, the development of planets, chemical evolution of matter, and the various places in the solar system where life exists or may exist.
ISBN 0-7614-1151-8
        1. Life—Origin—Juvenile literature. 2. Molecular evolution—Juvenile literature. [1. Life—Origin.] I. Title. II. Series
QH325.G35   2000   576.8'3—dc21   99—086435

Photo research by Linda Sykes Picture Research, Hilton Head, SC
Diagrams on pp. 13, 21, 23, 38, 41, 44, 46, 49, 50, 52, 56, 57, by Jeannine L. Dickey
Cover illustration:Corbis
Title page photo: Roy A. Gallant (geyser field of Dolina Geizeror, Kamchatka, Russia)
Photo credits: page 1 Roy A. Gallant; 6 Mark Moffett/Minden Pictures; 7 Jim Zuckerman/Corbis; 9 David Hardy/Photo Researchers; 10 Bodleian Library, Oxford University; 13 Museum of Oriental Antiquities, Istanbul, Turkey/Erich Lessing/Art Resource NY; 16 Kunsthistorisches Museum, Egyptian Collection, Vienna, Austria/Erich Lessing/Art Resource, NY; 30, 35, 37 The Granger Collection, New York; 32 Alinari/Art Resource, NY; 42, 53 Tui De Roy/ Bruce Coleman; 43 Kelvin Aitken/Peter Arnold Inc.; 54 Alan Detrick/ Photo Researchers; 60 Woods Hole Oceanographic Institution; 63 Jim White; 65, 70 Hubble Space Telescope/ NASA; 67 Courtesy of NASA; 68 both Courtesy of NASA/JPL/California Institute of Technology; 73 Hubble Space Telescope/T. A. Rector, B. Wolpa, M.Hanna KPNO 0.9-m Mosaic AURA/ NOAO/NSF

Printed in Hong Kong
6 5 4 3 2

To: Long-time friend and colleague Ed Kormondy

Out of the mists of time,
To put his troubled mind at ease
Man has spun a thousand fantasies,
And with them veiled his gaze
Against Nature's cold, purposeless ways.

Contents

One

In the Beginning

One of the most haunting questions we can ask is "How did life on planet Earth begin?" But maybe we should rephrase the question to broaden our search for answers. Perhaps the question should be "How may life begin, anywhere in the Universe?"

Critters Galore

The differences in life forms that have come and gone since time began for planet Earth boggle the imagination. There were those seemingly impossible, but wonderfully real, dinosaurs. There were critters with the strange-sounding names of trilobites, brachiopods, ammonoids, and cephalopods. And there were flightless birds. At the long end of life's clock, there are trees that have lived more

For millions of years life forms galore have crept, wiggled, scampered, and thundered across our planet, flown through its air, and swum through its oceans.

than a thousand years. At the short end are adult mayflies that live only a day.

There are more than 700,000 different kinds of insects and more than 350,000 kinds of beetles. More than 500 species of those whirring, buzzing, biting, stinging insect pests make the hottest and driest deserts of Africa their home. Inside sandstone rocks of Antarctica are thriving communities of microscopic critters—algae, fungi, and bacteria. Other such colonies have been found thriving deep down in Earth's rock crust where temperatures are high enough to kill most life. They wear the name cryptoendoliths, meaning "hidden dwellers inside rocks." Other colonies of organisms live in hot-water vents boiling up out of the deep seafloor. Others thrive in the perpetual dark and near-freezing water of Lake Vostok 13,000 feet (4,000 meters) beneath Antarctica's glacial ice. More than a dozen different kinds of bacteria live in the snow among the frigid peaks of the Himalayan Mountains at heights of 27,230 feet (8,300 meters). Fossil remains of ancient bacteria have been found 1.8 miles (3 kilometers) down in the planet's rock crust. All of these organisms, and countless millions more that have lived and died over the ages, grew and evolved from simple life forms that arose on Earth almost four billion years ago. That was only a billion or so years after planet Earth itself was formed.

Today's biologists have a pretty good idea of what those ancient ancestors were like because we find their fossils. They also have a pretty good idea of how those microscopic creatures gave rise to the bewildering circus of living things we find in the fossil record and those living today. But one nagging question has not yet been answered: Although we have tantalizing clues, how did those ancestors of early life forms come to be? The search for answers is not new. It has been going on ever since there have

Like clouds of black smoke billowing up out of the sea floor, deep ocean geysers bubble up hot mineral-rich water. This artist's view of one such geyser shows the abundance of plant and animal life associated with these cracks in the ocean floor called hydrothermal vents. When a vent becomes blocked, its community of plants and animals perishes.

been people to ask the question, and its history is one of the liveliest tales in the story of science.

Myths as Answers

Humans have a remarkable talent for inventing myths. Myths are fanciful stories made up to account for events in a timeless past, events that cannot, for the moment at least, be explained by natural causes. For example, to explain the Sun's daily flight across the sky, the ancient Greeks invented their Sun god Helios. Each morning he drove his golden chariot across the sky from his palace in the east. He then ended the day by disappearing below the western horizon.

An even more remarkable talent than inventing such myths is our willingness to believe in them.

Thousands of years ago, science as a way of seeking out explanations for how the world works did not exist. The natural causes of events such as volcanoes, earthquakes, lightning, and the planets' motions among the stars were unknown. They could only be guessed at. Yet such events had to be explained in some way. It was the myth-makers, sometimes religious leaders, some-times tribal elders who were looked to for answers. If they could-n't figure out the natural cause of a comet or an earthquake, they invented one. They created a myth, and the myth was handed

Myths and legends enrich the history and world views of most peoples who have ever lived. So popular was Alexander the Great as a seemingly superhuman warrior and conqueror that stories about his remarkable feats and adventures spread across all of Europe and Asia. He reportedly told of a land of lion-headed men, and another land where the people had their eyes and mouths in their breasts. Here, Alexander supposedly listens to another of his marvels, the Talking Tree.

down through the ages from one generation to the next. Myths are "counterfeit intelligence," according to the French philosopher Henri Bergson. They are substitute answers, pacifiers, that calm the mind until a real answer comes along. Myths are a kind of safety valve that calms the mind and keeps the world an orderly place.

No culture that we know of is without its myths, especially its creation myths that explain how life arose, especially human life.

The old myth-makers go back many thousands of years. How many, we shall never know. More than 5,000 years ago people living in the Middle East—called the Babylonians and Sumerians—had recorded their creation myths. But those myths must have been very old by the time they were first written down on clay tablets. A tradition of myth telling before the invention of writing must go back many more thousands of years.

We can arrange creation myths into three groups: (1) those in which Earth and its life were fashioned from the parts of some being's body, often a monster; (2) those that have Earth and its life being formed out of a world-ocean; and (3) those that have some supernatural being create itself and then create the world out of nothing.

P'an Ku One Chinese creation myth sets the stage for the creation of life with the creator-god P'an Ku, a grotesque being with horns, fangs, and a body covered with long hair. P'an Ku's first task as creator was to create order out of chaos. First he chiseled unorganized universal matter into the sky and land. Next he sculptured Earth's surface into mountains, valleys, and rivers. He then created the Sun, Moon, and stars. But to complete the setting, P'an Ku had to die. His skull became the perfect dome for the sky. His flesh became Earth's rich soil. His bones turned into the rocks, and from his blood came the rivers and seas. Trees and all other vegetation grew from his hair. The wind was his breath,

In addition to recording their creation myths on clay tablets, the Sumerians and Babylonians also recorded events in the night sky and kept track of items traded. The tablet shown here was recovered from the ancient city of Uruk, Mesopotamia and is some five thousand years old. The signs were made by pressing a stick "pen" into a soft clay tablet. The diagram shows the signs for bull, hand, barley, sheep, sun, and star.

thunder his voice, the Moon his right eye and the Sun his left, and his saliva turned into rain. People were created out of the lice, cockroaches, and other vermin that covered P'an Ku's body.

Several creation myths have the creator fashion people out of bits and pieces of his dead skin. In a Philippine tale, a white god with gold teeth kept rubbing his skin to make a mound of rubbed-off dead skin. When the mound was big enough, he made Earth out of it. He then turned the leftover bits into people.

Madumda The Pomo Indians of California tell of an old man named Madumda. He, too, scraped dead skin from his body and formed it into a ball. After eight days of sleep, Madumda awoke to find that the ball had grown to become Earth. He then hurled it off into space. He next created the Sun by blowing a spark from his pipe into the sky. Next he walked around Earth forming mountains, rocks, potatoes, rabbits, wolves, string beans, skunks, rattlesnakes, and other creatures. Finally, Madumda created people and left.

On a return visit to Earth Madumda found the people all fighting one another, so he decided to destroy them by causing a great flood. Then he created people for a second time, but these people also misbehaved, so Madumda killed them all with fire. He destroyed a third group of new people by causing an ice age to descend on them. Finally, he created a fourth group of people. To keep them from fighting each other, he made them speak different languages and spaced them all over Earth. Madumda then left Earth for the last time.

Ymir A Scandinavian creation myth tells of Ymir, the first living being. He was a giant fashioned out of frost. The chief god, Odin, and his two brothers kill Ymir. They make Earth out of his flesh, the oceans out of his blood, the mountains out of his bones, and the trees, grasses, and all other plants out of his hair. Ymir's huge skull forms the sky-dome above, and sparks within his head are scattered as the Sun, Moon, and stars. To this day, his brain broods over Earth as fog and dark rain clouds that hang low and that are common along certain coastal regions of Scandinavia. At Odin's command, dwarfs that live eternally underground and make beautiful jewels were created out of the maggots in Ymir's dead flesh. Later the gods created the first man, named Ask, out of an ash tree. Then they created the first woman, named Embla, out of an elm tree.

Among the most powerful creation myths are those of the two great prehistoric civilizations of Sumer and Egypt.

Atum The oldest of the Egyptian creation stories goes back some 6,000 years. It is an example of the second group of creation myths. In the beginning, the story goes, there was nothing but a world-ocean, called Nun. The first god, the Sun god Atum, created himself out of Nun. On rising out of the water, he said:

> *Out of the abyss I came to be*
> *But there was no place to stand.*

So Atum created a small mound of earth to support himself, and it became the world. Next he created Shu, god of the air, and Tefnut, goddess of moisture. From the union of Shu and Tefnut were born Geb, god of Earth, and Nut, goddess of the sky. Geb and Nut in turn produce the two gods Osiris and Set and the two goddesses Isis and Nepthys, from whom all the other Egyptian gods, and all people, were descended.

There are different versions of this Egyptian creation myth. Like many other such myths, the old myth-makers fashioned their tales partly on what they observed of the world. For instance, each year as the snows melted off the mountains in

Ethiopia, the Egyptian segment of the river Nile overflowed its banks from about July to October and flooded the surrounding land. After the flood waters drained away, silt carried by the river was left heaped up in little mounds—possibly a re-creation of the small mound of earth that Atum had created? Anyone who carefully examined these small hillocks of mud would see a variety of

In Egyptian mythology the goddess Nut was the daughter of the god Shu and the goddess Tefnut. This scene of Nut giving food and drink to the dead dates from the twenty-first Dynasty (1080 to 960 B.C.).

living organisms thriving under the warm Sun. For the Egyptians, here was the original source of the world.

The Sumerians had similar myths, and similar locations, including the Tigris-Euphrates river complex from which they could read similar events and reconstruct similar tales.

Yuchi Indians Cultures far removed from each other in time and place sometimes have creation myths whose main stories, if not the characters, are remarkably similar. Compare this creation myth of the Yuchi Indians of eastern Tennessee with that of the Egyptians (retold by Maria Leach in her book, *The Beginning*):

In the beginning there was only water. And someone said, "Who will make the land?"

"I will make the land," said Crawfish. And he dived down to the bottom of that great sea and stirred up the mud with his eight legs and his tail. And he took the mud in his fingers and made a little pile.

The owners of the mud down there said, "Who is stirring up the mud?" And they watched to see. But Crawfish kept stirring up the mud with his tail so that they could not see.

Every day Crawfish dived into the deep water and got a little more mud and put it on the pile. Day by day he piled it up. At last one day as he piled the mud on top of the pile, his hands came out of the water into the air! At last the land appeared above the water.

It was very soft, for it was mud.

Someone said, "Who will stretch out the land? Who will make it hard? Who will make it dry?"

Buzzard stretched out the earth and dried it. He spread his long wings and stretched it. He sailed over the earth; he spread it wide and dried it. Then, tiring, he

17

had to flap his wings and this made the mountains and valleys.

Someone said, "Who will make the light?"

Star said, "I will make light." But it was not enough. It was said, "Who will make more light?"

"I will make light," said Moon. But it was still night.

Someone said, "More light."

So Sun moved over into the east, and all at once a great beautiful light spread over the world. And then as sun moved from east to west, a drop of her blood fell and sank into the earth. From this blood and this earth came forth the first people, the Yuchi Indians. They called themselves Tsohaya, "People of the Sun," and every man who took this name had a picture of the Sun on his door.

A Break with the Past

In the absence of science, it was impossible for people of old to ask meaningful questions about the origin of life. For instance, chemistry deals with what things are made of and how one kind of matter reacts with another kind. That science was more than 2,000 years in the future. The very notion of atoms was unknown. It was not physics and chemistry and astronomy that set the world in motion and kept it humming. Instead it was an endless stream of gods, goddesses, spirits, demons, and other superstitious beliefs that provided order and a world view of things. Today we would call such a "world view" a model. As long as the model worked—explained things and reliably predicted the future— there was no reason to change it. But there was bound to come a time when the model failed to work, at least for some thinkers.

There probably was no one time or one place when the

model began to break down. There must have been nonbelievers among the old Sumerians, Babylonians, and Egyptians. They saw through the old myths and yearned for better explanations. They wanted to know what actually made the Moon go through phases, and they refused to cover their heads in fear during an eclipse of the Sun, and they refused to believe that the Sun, Moon, and stars held supernatural powers.

The time did come when such nonbelievers began to speak out boldly and challenge the gods. They were a new breed of thinkers who set up schools and won followers in that period of history we call the Golden Age of Greece, which began around 600 B.C.

Two

How the Greeks Discovered Nature

Ancient Greek religion, and the endless myths on which it was based, was a house of mirrors. It contained bits and pieces of religious lore from Crete, Egypt, Palestine, Babylonia, and parts of Asia. Yet it was out of this mixed-up background of superstitious beliefs that the early Greek philosophers emerged. Casting aside the old superstitions, they began to look on the formation of the world and its life as natural events, not work of the gods. It was these thinkers who began to lay the foundation of modern science.

More than two thousand years ago the great Greek thinkers imagined that all matter was mixtures of earth, air, fire, and water. They thought that these four basic "elements" were combined in certain ways to create the four "qualities" of matter. For example, fire and air combined to produce the quality of hot, and so on.

Searching for the "World-Stuff"

Today we would put the question this way: "What is *matter* made of?" The ancient Greeks spoke of the *world-stuff* and tried to imagine its composition. They were observers, not experimenters.

One such early thinker was Anaximander, who lived from 610 to 547 B.C. He spoke at length about an important "moist element" from which living creatures arose when the moist element was evaporated by the Sun. He further said that the first living things were trees and other plants. People did not come into being the way other animals did, he said. In support of his belief, he cited the long period of parental care needed by infants, and then very young children. Indeed, Anaximander said that human

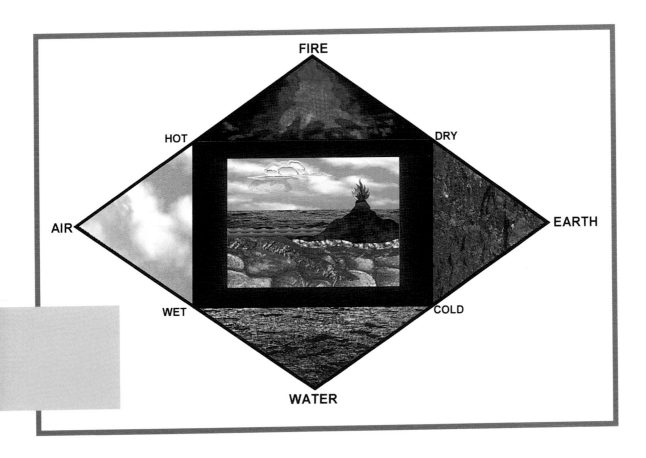

beings first arose inside fishes. After being reared that way long enough to be protected, they were finally cast ashore and took to the land. What observations could have led him to those conclusions are hard to imagine.

Other philosophers said that the world-stuff was water, or fire, or a breath-like substance called "pneuma." Thales, who lived from 625 to 547 B.C., taught that life arose from water because living organisms are made largely of water and depend on it for their well being. Around 450 B.C. a philosopher named Empedocles spoke of four "root elements." They were earth, air, fire, and water. When mixed in different combinations, he said, they formed all known substances—the seas, clouds, mountains, and living things. Any of those complex substances could then be turned back into the simpler root elements.

Aristotle, the greatest philosopher of ancient Greece, looked on the ideas of Empedocles with great favor. As a result, the four-root-element theory of the world-stuff was given an honored place in history for the next 2,000 years. Not until the year 1661 was the English chemist Robert Boyle to give us our present-day notion of the chemical elements. Aristotle even added a fifth element, or essence, of his own that has come down to us as the *quinta essentia*, meaning "fifth essence." The heavenly bodies must be made of purer stuff than earth-matter, he reasoned. In short, the stars and planets must be the "quintessence" of matter. He lived from 384 to 322 B.C.

Aristotle would have done better to adopt the ideas of an earlier Greek thinker who lived from 460 to 370 B.C. His name was Democritus, and he was the first atomist. Much of his thinking came from his teacher Leucippus. Democritus said that living things, and all other matter, were made up of *atoms*. His atoms were the smallest things that could exist. They were hard, came in many sizes, and could not be cut into smaller pieces. The word atom came from the Greek words a, which means "not," and *tomé*, which means "to cut." Atoms of metals were rough and heavy and stuck together. Atoms of water were slick and slid over one another easily. Atoms of air and fog were light and could drift about. Democritus imagined that his atoms were ageless, which meant that the Universe had always existed. And that suggested that life itself, in some form, might have always existed.

Before leaving the ancient Greek thinkers, we should make one important point about their world view. That view was very different from our own today. The Greeks did not make a sharp

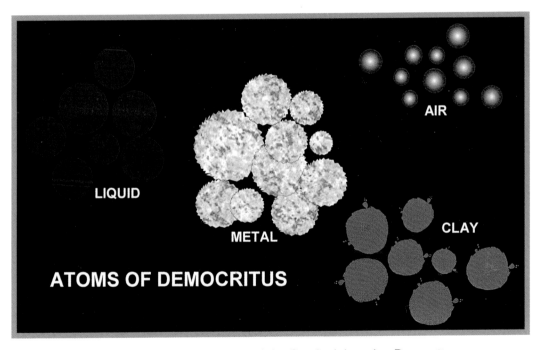

ATOMS OF DEMOCRITUS

All things are made of atoms, said the Greek philosopher Democritus— clouds, sheep, and rocks. He taught that atoms were the smallest possible pieces of matter. Some were rough and stuck together, like the atoms of metals and clay. Atoms of water were slippery and slid over each other. Atoms of air were light and spaced apart from one another.

distinction between nonliving parts of the Universe and living parts. They looked on the entire Universe as a living "organism," with plants, people, and other animals being only lesser organisms. Like the other giants of philosophy of ancient Greece, the great Aristotle had taught that living matter grew out of nonliving matter. They believed the origin of living matter from nonliving matter was going on all the time. That notion is called *spontaneous generation*, and it was to survive well into the 1600s. Aristotle firmly believed that worms and other creatures were made from the soil. He further believed that mosquitoes and fleas are generated spontaneously out of decaying matter and that fireflies arise out of morning dew.

The Golden Age of Greece came to a close around 150 B.C. The Greek states were conquered by the Romans, but the ideas spawned by the old Greek thinkers over the previous 500 years did not die. They continued to influence the thinking of scholars and others for the next fifteen hundred and more years.

One such person was the famous Roman poet Virgil, who lived from 70 to 19 B.C. In one of his poems he echoes a belief in spontaneous generation by providing a sort of recipe for making bees. "First, build a shed. Next, kill a bull during the first thaw of winter. Next, place the dead bull on branches with herbs inside the shed. Finally, wait for summer, at which time the decaying flesh of the bull will produce bees." Virgil said that if his instructions were closely followed, the bees would "swarm there and buzz, a marvel to behold."

Lucretius—the "Poet of Science"

The Roman philosopher-poet Lucretius lived around the time when Julius Caesar was emperor, about 50 B.C. In his long poem, *On the Nature of Things*, he scorns the old myths and urges his readers to look to natural causes to explain natural events. All such natural causes, he said, were associated with the atoms of Democritus.

Despite his voice of reason, he was a firm believer in spontaneous generation. In one of his poems he writes:

"And even now we see full many a breed
Of living creatures rise out of the earth
Begot by rains and by the genial warmth
The Sun doth shed."

Ever the naturalist and teacher, Lucretius instructs us on his first great principle: *Nothing can ever be created by divine power out of nothing.* The reason people are so gripped by fear, he says, is that they are ignorant of the natural causes for eclipses, comets, earthquakes, lightning, and volcanoes, for instance. Instead of looking for natural causes, he goes on, they take the easy way out and say that the gods control all such events. Our task, he says, is to look for causes that do not depend on the whims of the gods.

Lucretius then instructs us on his second great principle: *Nature arranges everything into its component atoms and never reduces anything to nothing.* Although living beings die and decay until they are gone from sight, he says, the atoms of which the living being was made are not destroyed. Nature reuses and rearranges them into other forms. Therefore, Lucretius concludes, "nothing returns to nothing. . . .Visible objects do not perish utterly, since nature rearranges one thing from another." That view is regarded as very sound science today.

Next, Lucretius challenges his readers to deny that atoms, which are too tiny to be seen, can exist. He cites strong winds that can capsize ships at sea and topple buildings. The winds, he tells us, are not magic performed by the gods. Instead, they are swarms

of atoms that can be felt but not seen. Odors and heat, he says, also are invisible substances made up of atoms in motion. Again, sound science.

Finally, Lucretius cites another of his grand principles: *It is in the highest degree unlikely that this earth and its sky is the only one to have been created.* Earth and all it contains, he informs us, was made by nature through the spontaneous and unplanned collisions of the many different kinds of atoms in the Universe. That is how "earth, and sea and sky and the races of living creatures" came to be. "On every ground," he goes on to say, "you must admit that there exist elsewhere other groupings of matter similar to those on earth. . . . You have the same natural force to group them in any place just as they have been grouped here. You are bound, therefore, to admit that in other parts of the Universe there are other earths and various tribes of men and breeds of beasts."

In Lucretius we find a voice that echoes many ideas of the old Greek masters that were to be reborn many centuries later by modern science.

By the year A.D. 380, the Christian church had become the only approved religion of Rome. Church leaders would not tolerate any views about the origin of life other than that of divine creation as described in the Bible: God created the Universe out of nothing and created all life. Earth occupied the central position in the Universe. It also stood motionless at the center. Further, man occupied the central position among all of God's creatures. And that was that.

Or was it?

In the 1500s and 1600s astronomers upset the church-supported belief that Earth was the center of the Universe. With Earth toppled from its privileged position in the heavens, scientists began to wonder about Lucretius's old notion that there must be other worlds out there and other forms of life. If so, then how did *that* life originate?

The ghost of Lucretius had returned to haunt those who still looked to the gods of creation. He had said that "nature is free and uncontrolled by proud masters and runs the Universe by herself without the aid of gods." If that were so, then what were those "natural causes" that could explain the "natural event" of the creation of living things—on Earth or elsewhere in the Universe? We must remember that the sciences of chemistry and biology had only wobbly foundations in the 1500s. More had to be learned about the atoms of Democritus and how they joined to form different substances to provide meaning to Lucretius's idea of natural causes. Meanwhile, the notion of spontaneous generation seemed quite natural and acceptable.

Three

Spontaneous Generation

How to Make Mice

J. B. van Helmont was a most unusual man. A Flemish doctor, chemist, and physicist, he lived from 1577 to 1644. He was a mixture of scientist and believer in certain ideas that today strike us as, well, not very scientific. For one thing, he was a mystic, someone who believes that knowledge can be obtained from the spirit world. He claimed that all knowledge was the gift of God. He also believed in spontaneous generation, but so did such geniuses as the English physicist Isaac Newton, the French philosopher René Descartes, and a number of other well known scientists of the time. Helmont even wrote a recipe for creating mice:

> "If a dirty undergarment is squeezed in through the mouth of a vessel containing wheat, within a few days (say 21) a ferment drained from the garment, and transformed by the smell of the grain, encrusts the wheat

with a skin and turns it into mice. . . . And, what is more remarkable, the mice from corn and undergarments are neither weanlings nor sucklings nor premature, but they jump out fully formed."

It's hard to imagine what direct observations could have led Helmont to the conclusion that mice could arise spontaneously out of dirty underwear. But, being an intelligent man, he must have had some reason for believing as he did, as did others before him. Sometimes a perfectly good observation can suggest the wrong conclusion. The ancient Egyptians were convinced that mice were generated spontaneously from mud. That conclusion probably came from their observation of sudden plagues of mice occurring each year after the Nile flooded its banks and left vast deposits of mud.

On the plus side of his career, Helmont invented the chemical term gas (from the Greek word for chaos). He also identified the gas carbon dioxide. He rejected the four root "elements" of Empedocles and Aristotle and instead believed there were only two such root substances—air and water. But the English chemist Robert Boyle, who lived from 1627 to 1691, said that only four so-called elements could not even begin to account for all the chemical changes that take place in nature. It was Boyle who discovered the true nature of chemical elements: *An element is a substance that cannot be broken down into or built up from simpler substances by chemical means.* Today we know of about 120 different elements. Elements most important to living matter include carbon, hydrogen, oxygen, nitrogen, sodium, potassium, and phosphorus.

In spite of Boyle's many experiments that helped turn chemistry into a sound science, many chemists of the time still clung to

The English chemist Robert Boyle, who lived around 1660 swept away the old idea of earth, air, fire, and water as the four basic "elements." He felt that many more than four elements were needed to account for all of the chemical changes we observe in nature.

the old earth-air-fire-water scheme approved by Aristotle. Old ideas often die hard. Yet even those chemists eventually came to look to the laboratory and experiments, not the philosophers, for enlightenment.

Redi Attacks Spontaneous Generation

About the time Boyle was experimenting with gases, a number of physicians were doing experiments to test the notion of spontaneous generation. The 1600s ushered in an era of experimenting that poked holes in many of Aristotle's ideas.

One such physician was the Italian Francesco Redi, who lived from 1626 to 1697. One belief popular during his time was that maggots are generated spontaneously by rotting meat. Maggots are those tiny white wormlike critters that hatch from fly eggs and then turn into adult houseflies.

Redi hit on an idea for an experiment to test the belief that maggots are created out of decaying flesh. The idea came to him as he watched what happened to three dead snakes he had tossed into a box.

Day by day he examined the snakes to see what happened to them as they decayed. One day he noticed flies hovering over them. Three days later he saw maggots crawling over the rotting meat and eating it. Soon, all that was left of the snakes were their bones. Redi next put some of the maggots into a jar and observed them. After 19 days they began to form into hard balls, and eight days later adult flies broke out of the tiny balls, or what we now call pupal cases. During Redi's time, the life cycles of insects were not very well known, although Redi did know that caterpillars went through a stage when they spin a cocoon.

Watching the maggots gave Redi an idea for an experiment. Such an idea in science is called a *hypothesis*. Here was Redi's

At the time Boyle was helping to lay the foundation stones of modern chemistry, the old alchemists were concocting brews of liquids and metals in one failed attempt after another to make gold. For centuries they had blended mercury, lead, copper, and other substances, thinking that one day they would discover the secret of making gold and silver.

Today it is hard for us to imagine how such an idea as a "people tree," a tree that bore people as its fruit, could have been imagined. This drawing is based on an old woodcut from a Turkish history of India.

hypothesis: *Maggots are not created out of decaying meat. Instead, flies lay their eggs on the rotting flesh. Maggots then hatch from the eggs. Finally the maggots turn into adult flies.*

Redi designed a very simple experiment. He placed pieces of decaying meat into four jars—snake flesh in one jar, a dead eel in another, flesh from a calf in a third, and some rotting fish in the fourth. He did not cap the jars, but left them open to the air. Then he prepared four more jars exactly the same way, except he did cap the tops of these jars with cloth that would keep flies out but let air circulate inside the jars. Each day he examined the jars and noticed that flies were entering and leaving the four open jars, but they couldn't enter the second set of jars. A few days later he saw that maggots were swarming over the meat in the open jars but not a single maggot was seen in the covered jars. Redi was able to conclude that flies are not generated spontaneously by decaying meat. Flies are generated only by other flies.

The idea that living things were produced only by other living things of the same kind became a major principle in biology. It is called *biogenesis*.

Redi's work, as important as it was, did not disprove spontaneous generation. However, similar experiments with other organisms done by other medical scientists went a long way toward putting spontaneous generation on trial. But then something happened to make the idea popular again. Microscopes came into popular use among biologists. When they did, they opened a bewildering new world of organisms never seen before.

Van Leeuwenhoek's Animalcules

The next major actor in the drama of spontaneous generation was the Dutch experimenter Antonie van Leeuwenhoek. He lived from 1632 to 1723. It was his work that gave spontaneous generation a new lease on life, although he himself was a firm disbeliever in the idea. Leeuwenhoek was one of those unusual individuals without any scientific training who became famous for his scientific work. His fame came from designing and making microscopes and then showing the world in great detail the marvels they revealed. By the time he died, he had made 147 microscopes and was honored by being elected a Fellow of England's famed Royal Society.

Here is how Leeuwenhoek described his surprise and wonder on examining water in which he had mixed pepper and let stand for three weeks: "I saw in it, to my great wonder, an incredible

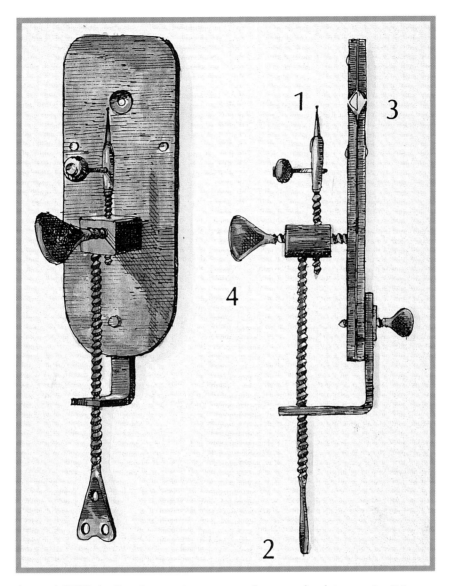

Around 1700 the Dutch experimenter van Leeuwenhoek gave scientists their first view of organisms too small to be seen by the unaided eye. His microscopes were crude by today's standards but could magnify tiny life forms 200 times actual size. The specimen to be observed was placed at the tip at (1), was positioned vertically by turning the lower screw at (2), and moved toward or away from the lens at (3) by turning the shorter screw at (4).

number of little animals of diverse kinds; some were 3 or 4 times as long as broad, but their thickness did, in my estimation, not much exceed that of the hair of a louse. They have a very pretty motion, often tumbling about and sideways. . . ."

On reading his vivid descriptions, biologists began to wonder where the hundreds of microscopic "animalcules," as he called them, came from. Since they appeared so simple, maybe they did not obey the law of biogenesis. Maybe they *did* arise from nonliving matter. After all, if a few strands of hay were placed in pure water, a few days later the water was swarming with tiny creatures! Where did they come from? The whole argument over spontaneous generation suddenly opened up again.

Some scientists argued one way, others the other way. Some mixed hay with water and thoroughly boiled the mixture. Half the fluid was then drained off and sealed in a second container. The other half of the fluid was left open to the air. Several days later the fluids from both containers were examined. The fluid that had been sealed off from the air did not contain any animalcules. The fluid that had been left open to the air swarmed with critters. Those who argued against spontaneous generation said that the animalcules found in the fluid of the open container had drifted in from the air. Those who argued for spontaneous generation claimed that the reason no animalcules were found in the fluid of the sealed container was that some *life force* in the fluid had been destroyed. Neither side would admit defeat, and so matters stood until the 1800s.

Pasteur Kills Spontaneous Generation

The death blow to the spontaneous generation of microscopic organisms was delivered in 1862 by the famous French chemist Louis Pasteur. The renowned French Academy of Sciences offered a prize to the winner of a debate over spontaneous generation. Pasteur, who lived from 1822 to 1895, won easily, and the study of the origin of life was changed forever.

Pasteur's fame actually came from other types of work. He studied the causes of several diseases and developed protection, in the form of vaccines, against them. Two such ailments were anthrax and rabies. His vaccine against rabies—caused by the bite of a "mad" dog, and other animals, instantly made him world famous.

His simple experiment that dealt the death blow to the spontaneous generation of microscopic organisms was so convincing

In 1862 the French chemist Louis Pasteur changed the study of the origins of life forever. His experiments dealt a death blow to the theory of spontaneous generation, which had been favored since Aristotle's time.

that no one could fault it. First, he collected samples of air, examined them under a microscope, and showed that the air contains many microscopic organisms—bacteria—that cling to dust particles floating in the air. He called them "germs of the lowest organisms." Next he poured meat broth into a glass container. He then heated the container and stretched out the softened glass into the shape of a swan's neck with an opening only

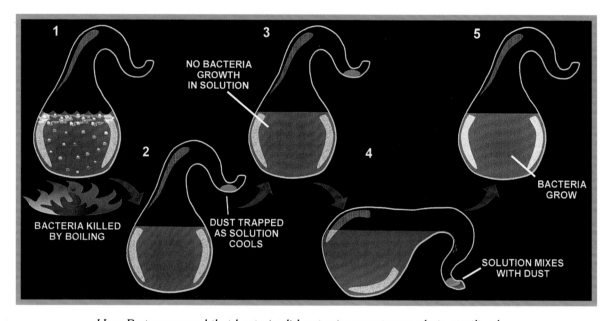

How Pasteur proved that bacteria did not arise spontaneously in sterilized broth but entered the broth from the air and so infected it: (1) He boiled the broth to kill all bacteria in the broth and inside the glass flask. (2) Bacteria clinging to dust in the air were able to enter the flask through the pin hole entrance but became trapped in the curved section and so were not able to reach the broth. (3) Left in storage for several days or weeks, the broth remained free of the bacteria trapped in the curved pocket of the flask. (4) When the flask was tipped so that some of the broth spilled into the trap area, bacteria quickly mixed with the spilled broth. (5) When the broth spilled into the trap was allowed to flow back into the main broth supply, the bacteria immediately infected all the broth.

the size of a pinhole. He then boiled the broth to kill any organ-isms in the broth and inside the container.

Once cooled, and sitting on a shelf for a day, a week, or a month, the broth remained free of any microscopic organisms. Pasteur knew because he would break open one such jar and examine the broth under a microscope. No animalcules. The reason was that the dust particles with germs clinging to them got stuck to the inside of the narrow swan-neck tube end of the container and never could reach the broth at the bottom. Pasteur then tilted the container so that some of the broth ran down and sloshed around near the pinhole entrance, where it picked up bacteria. The broth, now polluted with bacteria, was then allowed to run back into the main part of the container and mix with the clean broth. The bacteria soon multiplied and formed a thriving colony in the broth.

Once and for all, Pasteur had put an end to spontaneous generation.

Even so, biologists by the end of the 1800s still had to face a gnawing question: Where did Leeuwenhoek's animalcules—those simplest and most primitive of all known living matter—come from, IF they were not generated spontaneously and IF biogenesis was the rule of life? Before we can answer that question we must turn back the pages of Earth's history to the time the planet was formed.

Four

Earth in its Youth

About a hundred years before Pasteur lived and was asking questions about microscopic organisms, the German philosopher Immanuel Kant was asking questions about planet Earth's beginnings. The basic plan he outlined in 1755, remarkably, is the one today's astronomers favor, although Kant's plan lacked the many details we now have.

A Planet is Born

The Sun and its nine planets were formed some 4.6 billion years ago out of a huge cloud of gas and cosmic dust. The gas was

Earth and the other planets formed right along with the Sun. It all started (top left) when a giant cloud of gas and dust collapsed in on itself. Packed ever tighter, the central region of the cloud heated up and became the Sun. Meanwhile, lumps of rock, metal, and ices (top right) collected into globes that became the planets. Eventually the left-over gas and dust was swept up by the Sun and planets and space within the Solar System was so swept clean.

mostly hydrogen while the dust was clumps of atoms of rocky matter, metals, and ices. Over more than a hundred million years that mixture of gases, rock, ices, and metals came together as mountain-size objects called *planetesimals*. Over millions of years more, countless thousands of those planetesimals collided and clumped together as the planets, each orbiting about the large central mass of matter that became the Sun.

The truly remarkable thing about all of this is not that it happened, but that, in the words of the late astronomer Carl Sagan, "a mindless selective process can convert chaos into order." That

No one knows what conditions were like on Earth nearly four billion years ago. But it now seems likely that sometime between 3.5 billion and four billion years ago complex molecules were building structures that would soon blossom into the earliest living matter. But under what conditions was that living matter born, and what conditions allowed it to thrive? The

thought applies not only to the organization of matter and energy that formed the nonliving matter of the Solar System, but that formed living matter as well.

Over those millions of years, Earth swept up more and more planetesimals, and so grew in mass and in size. All of those planetesimals crashing into Earth helped heat up the planet until it became a molten globe. Gravity caused the heavier matter of iron and nickel to sink into the core region. Lighter materials, such as the silicate rocks, floated up to the surface. There they

naturalist Charles Darwin pictured a "warm little pond." Some scientists today picture a harsh world where the oceans were covered with a thousand feet (300 meters) of ice. But beneath that ice on the deep sea floor were hot vents bubbling up a rich supply of mineral compounds out of which the first living matter was formed.

slowly cooled and hardened into the planet's rock crust. Other materials included the elements hydrogen, helium, aluminum, gold, uranium, sulfur, and phosphorus. Many of those cosmic icebergs we call comets also crashed into young Earth and so helped provide the planet with water.

Meanwhile, many gases, including water vapor, boiled up through volcanic vents in the rock crust and so started a build-up of Earth's early atmosphere. But that atmosphere was very different from the one we have today. It included lots of hydrogen, water vapor, nitrogen, carbon monoxide, and carbon dioxide, along with smaller amounts of methane, ammonia, and hydrogen sulfide. There also were the poisonous substances cyanide and formaldehyde. There was hardly any oxygen, the gas of life. Later, we will find out how an oxygen revolution came about, and its importance to life on the planet.

Eventually, as the rock crust cooled, water from countless geysers spouting boiling water and steam into the air also cooled and collected as the first shallow, warm seas. By about 3.9 billion years ago, a cool solid crust of rock floated on a vast underground

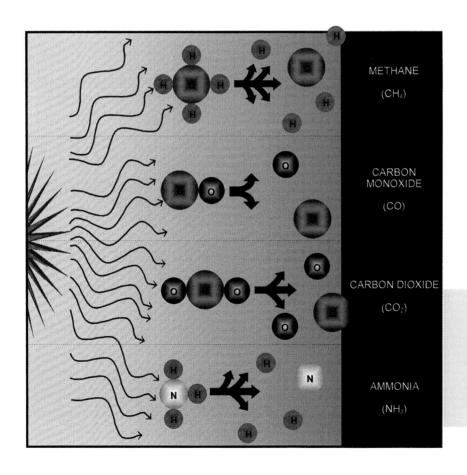

METHANE

(CH₄)

CARBON
MONOXIDE

(CO)

CARBON DIOXIDE

(CO₂)

AMMONIA

(NH₃)

ocean of molten rock, which still exists today. As Earth's land surface was changing, so was its atmosphere. Energy from the Sun was breaking down ammonia gases into free hydrogen and nitrogen. Methane was broken down into carbon and hydrogen. Water vapor was being changed into free hydrogen and oxygen. But the free hydrogen was so light that most of it escaped the planet's gravitational grip. The scene was then set for what biologists now think were the early steps leading to the origin of life.

The Cell: The Basic Unit of Life

Before looking at the work of some of the biologists who have made it their life's work to study how life on Earth might have begun, we should first talk about living *cells*.

Biologists regard the cell as the basic unit of life. And they regard life as *what matter does*. Your body is made up of some ten quadrillion (10,000,000,000,000,000) cells of about a hundred different kinds. Some help digest food. Others enable you to think. Cells are specialized to perform all the tasks that the body performs. Most cells are smaller than the dot over this letter i. Yet the tiniest cell is able to carry out all of the essential life functions that you yourself carry out. Now that is a remarkable thing and a good reason for you to study biology some day.

As Earth's early land surface changed, so did its atmosphere. Energy from the Sun (left) broke down methane (top) into free hydrogen and carbon atoms. It also broke down carbon monoxide and carbon dioxide into free oxygen and carbon atoms. Ammonia (bottom) was broken down into free hydrogen and nitrogen atoms. Water vapor (not shown) was changed into free hydrogen and oxygen. But the free hydrogen atoms were so light that most of them escaped the planet's gravitational grip.

A cell is a sac of fluid that contains various parts that *serve* the cell in special ways, just as your body has a stomach, liver, lungs, and other special parts that serve you in special ways. Each cell is held together within a membrane jacket that has very tiny holes. The holes let the cell expel wastes to the outside and allow the cell to take in certain atoms that it needs as food and as parts for repair. Inside the cell, the atoms and clusters of atoms, called *molecules*, are wonderfully organized, and their activities are kept in order by the cell's control center, the *nucleus*. Outside the cell,

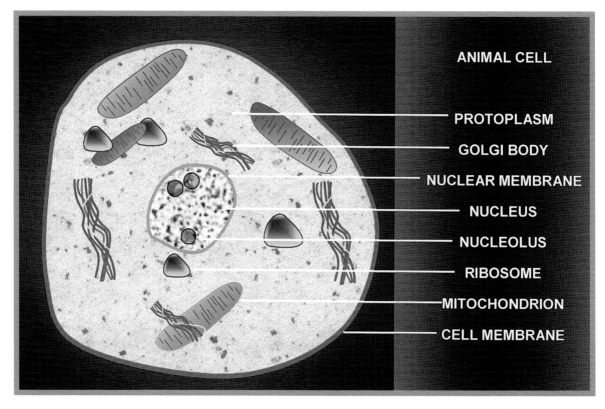

ANIMAL CELL

PROTOPLASM

GOLGI BODY

NUCLEAR MEMBRANE

NUCLEUS

NUCLEOLUS

RIBOSOME

MITOCHONDRION

CELL MEMBRANE

A typical animal cell with some of its many parts (called organelles) that help it carry out all of the life processes that your body does. Your body is made up of about a hundred different kinds of cells, each kind designed to carry out different functions.

the world of atoms and molecules is disorderly, so the cell membrane is protection against that disorder. Without its membrane, a cell would die instantly. The cell is so marvelously complex and orderly that biologists are quite baffled by it. They also are hard-put to explain how the first cells evolved from the chaos of atoms and molecules that floated about in Earth's warm seas almost four billion years ago.

The Chemical Evolution of Matter

Now that we know at least something about what a living cell is and what it does, we are in a better position to search for an answer to how they came about. So we'll continue our story after Pasteur's important work with what he called germs, or *microbes*. We move the clock ahead from the late 1800s to the year 1924. The place is Russia, and the person a chemist named A. I. Oparin. Like others before him, Oparin was fascinated by the puzzle of how the first things that we call "living" arose on Earth.

He pictured it all starting when simple chemicals in Earth's primitive atmosphere and in the planet's early seas joined quite naturally and formed more complex molecules and groupings of molecules he called *coacervates*. Such molecular clustering can be demonstrated in the laboratory. Such a cluster has an electric charge that keeps surrounding water molecules at a certain distance, which forms a shell around the cluster. The shell is similar to a cell's protective membrane. A coacervate droplet can attract certain molecules outside its shell and bring them inside. But the molecules from the outside must be exactly the right shape to attach and fit onto the molecule group inside. Oparin viewed such action as "growth," since the coacervate clump became increasingly large and more complex with each addition.

Oparin said there must have been many different kinds of

coacervate groups in Earth's early seas. He pictured the more successful droplets growing so large that they became unstable and broke into smaller droplets. Those smaller droplets then took in "nutrient" molecules from the outside and grew. Were Oparin's coacervate droplets alive? He has said that "there is no *fundamental* difference between a living organism and lifeless matter." Recall that physicians of Redi's time searched for some kind of "life force" that distinguished living matter from nonliving matter. They never found one, nor have biologists since Redi's time been able to find one. Oparin's coacervates have been called prebiological cells. They take in nutrients from the outside, they have a protective membrane of sorts, they grow, and they can reproduce more of their kind. Do they qualify as living matter or not?

What evidence do we have that complex molecules like those found in animals and plants actually could have been formed naturally nearly four billion years ago?

To answer that question our story jumps ahead to the early 1950s and Stanley Miller, who was a student at the University of Chicago. He designed an experiment to find out what kinds of complex molecules essential for life might have been built up in Earth's primitive atmosphere.

Through a closed system of glass tubing Miller circulated a mixture of hydrogen, methane, ammonia, and water vapor, all present in Earth's early atmosphere. He then set off electric discharges to the gases to make them react with each other. In Earth's early atmosphere, lightning discharges and ultraviolet radiation would have been energy sources to ignite chemical reactions in the air and in shallow seas. The water vapor in Miller's glass tubing condensed as "rain," and the other gases dissolved in the rainwater. A week later he drew off some of the liquid and examined it. A number of complex molecules had been built

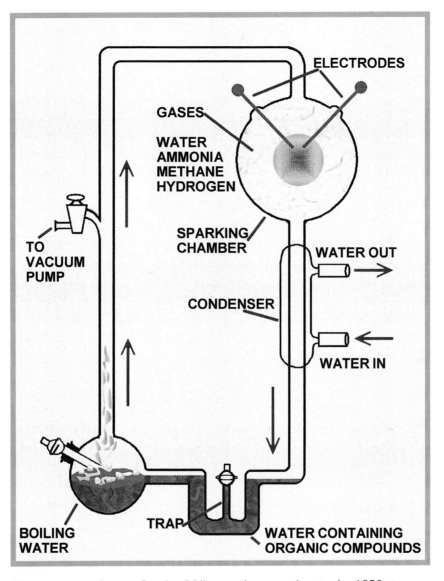

The apparatus chemist Stanley Miller used as a student in the 1950s in experiments to investigate the chemical origins of life. He set off electric discharges in a mixture of hydrogen, methane, ammonia, and water vapor—gases thought to have been in Earth's early atmosphere. Imagine his surprise when he found that he had produced a number of chemicals essential to life. Among them were amino acids, which are the building blocks of proteins.

up, and they were molecules essential to all living things. Among them were those molecules known as *amino acids*, which are the building blocks of protein. One of our cells' chief tasks is to make protein molecules. Those molecules are then used as food and building parts for a cell.

Miller's molecules of life were a far cry from a living cell, but they were essential parts of all living things.

Soon after Miller's experiments, another American investigator, Sydney Fox, produced tiny cell-like structures that he called *microspheres*. They were clusters of amino acids, molecules very much like protein, and they enclosed themselves in a sort of membrane. Miller and Fox showed that young Earth could have quite naturally produced the amino acids needed to make protein,

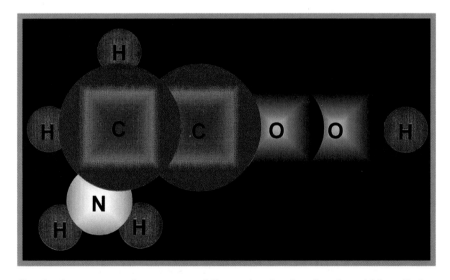

Our bodies contain about twenty different kinds of molecules of life called amino acids. The simplest one is glycine. It is made up of two atoms of carbon, two of oxygen, five of hydrogen, and one of nitrogen. These common and essential building blocks of living matter are not Earth-bound but are space travelers. They have been found in meteorites, for example.

and then the very protein itself. And all without the help of any living thing!

Chemical Evolution—Part II

What happened to those prebiological cells that took in ready-made "food" molecules from the outside? With more and more such cells gobbling up nutrient molecules from the environment, we can imagine that a time would come when nutrient molecules might be in short supply. What then?

We can picture a more efficient breed of prebiological cell—one that could take in smaller and simpler molecules from the outside and then assemble them inside as food and building materials. Such smart prebiological cells would have a great advantage over their less able relatives who depended on ready-made food molecules from a primeval Burger King rather than making their food from scraps of simple molecules. The advantage would be an unlimited supply of simpler molecules. All the green plants around us today do just what those smart prebiological cells did. Green plants take in molecules of water vapor and carbon dioxide from the air through their leaves. They then use the energy of sunlight to combine those simple molecules into complex molecules of the sugar glucose. That process is called *photosynthesis*. Glucose is food not only for green plants but for all the animals that eat green plants, including us.

We are now left with this question: IF the idea of smart pre-biological cells comes close to what actually happened nearly four billion years ago, then what happened next that led to the simplest biological cells? Such cells were what we today call bacteria. Bacteria are found by the trillions virtually everywhere. They drift about in the air ready to infect us with diseases, as Pasteur proved. They live in soil and make it fertile. They live in the lake-bottom ooze without oxygen. And they live on and in our bodies, where they help digest our food. Your body is home to billions of bacterial cells. Their environment inside your body is more like what Earth was like nearly four billion years ago than what it is like today.

The ability of bacterial cells to reproduce is astonishing. One cell simply divides into two new cells. Where there was one bacterium, 20 minutes later there are two. And 20 minutes after that there are four. In just one day a single bacterium can give rise to a million new cells just like itself. Bacteria and other microscopic life forms probably make up half of all living matter on Earth today.

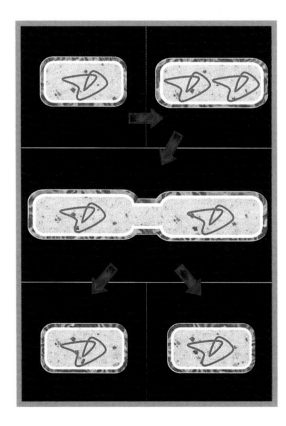

Bacterial cells make more bacteria by simply dividing in two. A single bacterium (top left) first makes an exact copy of its genetic material (top right). The cell is then pinched off (middle) in two new bacterial cells, each identical to one another. The entire process of division takes about twenty minutes.

They look like small rounded boulders but actually are half-dead, half-alive rocklike communities of half a billion or more bacteria called stromatolites. They are survivors of Earth's first living communities that thrived around the globe 3.5 billion years ago. Among the few that remain are these along the shore of Shark Bay in Western Australia. The top few inches are a squishy mat crowned with cyanobacteria that thrive in oxygen and sunlight. Beneath is a layer of different bacteria that can stand some sunlight and a little oxygen; and beneath that layer is a base layer of bacteria that thrive only in the dark and where there is no oxygen. Mud and fine sand become trapped in the living mat. To survive, the bacteria keep rising up through the sediments, and so the stromatolite "grows" larger. The central region of each stromatolite is an ever-growing core of sediments turned to stone as they are bound into a solid mass by reacting with calcium carbonate in the sea water. During the millions of years the stromatolites ruled, bacteria probably were the only life forms on the planet.

We have fossil evidence from southwestern Greenland that bacterial cells were around at least 3.86 billion years ago. The biologist Lynn Margulis speaks of a time she calls The Age of Bacteria, probably 2.5 billion years ago. Broad blankets of bacteria stretched from horizon to horizon and colored the land and lakes and rivers green, brown, yellow, and purple. For the first few billion years bacteria may have been the only living organisms on Earth. Eventually, they gave rise to all other life forms. Margulis likes to remind us of our true origins: "We always think we came

Rainbows of colorful bacteria adorn the hot springs of Yellowstone National Park. The bacteria serve as thermometers because those of certain colors live within certain ranges of water temperature. Biologist Anna-Louise Reysenbach, of Rutgers University, believes that the microbes found in Yellowstone's hot springs are the "closest relatives to the original ancestor of life we've found so far."

from the apes. But our cells really come from the bacterial world." And a sobering thought is that for three-quarters of its span on Earth, life evolved almost entirely as microorganisms.

The Oxygen Revolution

Among that seemingly endless carpet of bacteria, some took in ready-made food molecules from the environment. Others made their own food by combining hydrogen with carbon dioxide in the air in the process of photosynthesis. As they did, they brought on the greatest natural "catastrophe" that Earth has ever experienced. It was the introduction into the environment of huge amounts of a gas that was poisonous to nearly all cells living at the time—oxygen. Oxygen, so precious to most organisms living today, is given off as a "waste" gas during photosynthesis.

As more and more oxygen kept pouring into the air, trouble started. Unless an organism is packaged so that it is protected from oxygen, it will be poisoned by the gas. Free oxygen quickly combines with and breaks down the complex molecules of living matter. It breaks down vitamins. It destroys proteins and destroys cell membranes, killing a cell instantly. Many populations of bacteria were wiped out by this new gas. But those that had taken up life in mud flats and swamp bottoms avoided the gas and survived. Such bacteria remained unchanged through the ages and are wildly successful to this day. They are the *cyanobacteria* that form the scum on swimming pools and coat shower curtains. Certain other bacteria learned to live with oxygen. They even came to depend on it. Life would never be the same again. The stage was set for those simplest life forms to evolve into complex cells, then colonies of cells, and the overwhelming variety of animals and plants that have come and gone over the hundreds of millions of years in Earth's history.

OZONE
LAYER

The ozone layer in Earth's atmosphere is made up of heavy molecules of three atoms of oxygen each. The ordinary oxygen we breathe is made up of molecules of two atoms each. The ozone layer blocks high-energy ultraviolet rays (dark red) from reaching Earth's surface but lets the low-energy ultraviolet rays (pink) through. That low-energy radiation is what causes sunburn. Without the ozone layer, the high-energy ultraviolet radiation would kill most life forms on the planet.

Margulis is convinced that the early complex cells of about two billion years ago were built up by simpler cells merging into a single individual. She explains it this way: First, a bacterium that thrived in a hot environment and relied on sulfur instead of oxygen for energy merged with a swimming bacterium. Since it would have been poisoned by oxygen, this new individual lived in mud, rock crevices, and puddles, where there was little or no oxygen. Next, a bacterium that was an expert oxygen user merged with the two-part individual that could not use oxygen. So the combination heat-lover, swimmer, and oxygen breather became a still more talented individual. But the merger didn't stop there. The newer three-part individual was unable to make its own food, but it soon learned how. On gobbling up bright green bacteria as food, it could not digest them. The result was that the green bacterium lived inside the three-part individual and so gave rise to a still more efficient four-part individual. It was

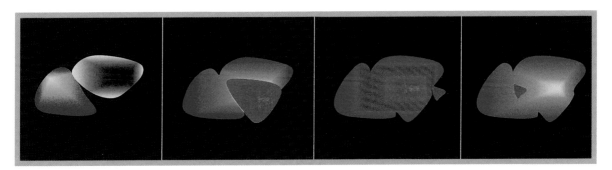

Join and gobble up is the way biologist Lynn Margulis thinks primitive life forms evolved into more complex forms. At left two cells, each with a special talent, merge into a single individual which now has both talents. Next the two-part individual joins with a third cell and so picks up that cell's special talent. The three-part individual then gobbles up still another cell (green) with the special talent of making its own food by combining water and carbon dioxide in the presence of sunlight. That talent makes the new four-part individual a supercell.

more efficient because the new superbacterium was able to carry out photosynthesis and make glucose-food. Margulis calls this process of simpler cells, or cell parts, merging and creating a new and better individual *symbiogenesis*. Although the idea is about a hundred years old, her approach to it is new, and many biologists are impressed by her new-age thinking.

So, somewhere at some time in Earth's early history, complex chemical clumps evolved into the first biological cells. Perhaps they were Oparin's coacervates, or Fox's microspheres, or something like them. Those simple organisms then merged into more complex ones, as imagined by Margulis. Some biologists doubt that we will ever know all the details of how that immense gulf between prebiological and biological cells was spanned. But according to the biochemist Cyril Ponnamperuma: "There is no reason to doubt that we shall rediscover one by one the physical and chemical conditions that once determined and directed the course of chemical evolution. We may even reproduce the intermediate steps in the laboratory."

Until fairly recently, biologists had limited their search for Earth's first living matter to the planet's warm and shallow seas and primeval ooze. But in the 1970s and 1980s oceanographers began making a series of surprising discoveries. Those discoveries suggest to some that Earth's first living creatures might have evolved not on warm little ponds but out of materials boiling up out of the deep ocean floor.

Five

From the Seafloor to the Stars

At first, the idea might seem crazy. But then, maybe not. Maybe life on Earth first arose at the bottom of the oceans and later moved onto the land. Or perhaps primitive life forms, or complex building blocks of living matter, evolved on another planet, then drifted across space from the stars and "infected" Earth.

Smokers as Cradles of Life?

In 1977, the American geologist and oceanographer Robert Ballard was exploring the seafloor between South America and the Galapagos Islands. He was studying the Galapagos Mid-Ocean Ridge, part of a seafloor mountain chain that snakes its way for thousands of miles around the globe. The ridge is formed as hot, molten rock from deep within Earth wells up through cracks in the seafloor and continually builds the ridge system.

Ballard was studying the seafloor by lowering a sled equipped with a camera to a depth of 8,000 feet (2,440 meters). Scientists found it hard to believe what the films revealed. There were shoe-sized clams, strange-looking crabs, and enormous tan and red tube worms six feet (1.8 meters) long. What were such organisms doing living at such great depths, where most of the ocean floor is without life? The photographs also showed stacks like chimneys rising to heights of 165 feet (50 meters). Bellowing out of the chimneys were clouds of black smokelike matter. They were powerful undersea geysers belching out hot minerals that included

Underwater sled with deep-sea camera used by oceanographer Robert Ballard to photograph previously unknown colonies of marine organisms living at depths of 8,000 feet (2,440 meters).

iron, zinc, tin, copper, silver, and sulfur. Such minerals color some of the smokers black. These cracks in the ocean floor are called *hydrothermal vents*. Their geyser outpourings, heated by the molten rock less than a half mile (less than a kilometer) below, reach temperatures ranging anywhere from 86°F (30°C) to almost 1,000°F (540°C).

The chimneys of solidified minerals may rise as slim columns, or they may simply be clumps. Depending on the kinds of minerals they contain, they can range in color from orange to green to brown, or white. One oceanographer said he saw "blizzards" of bacteria pouring out of one chimney. He called them "snowblowers." The minerals serve as food for the bacteria, and in turn the bacteria serve as food for shrimp and clams and the tube worms. Crabs eat the tube worms, and a certain species of fish eats the crabs and other critters that live around the hot geyser.

The animals and plants that make these ocean-bottom hot vents their home are not like any other organisms on Earth. The main thing that sets them apart from other life forms is that they do not depend on the energy of sunlight. They live in the eternal dark of the seafloor. Their energy sources are the nutrients that boil up out of the hot vents. When one of these undersea geysers stops erupting, its community of plants and animals perishes. The life span of a typical hydrothermal vent community may be only 50 years or so.

Scientists now think that water of all the oceans flows through this seafloor plumbing system every three million years or so. This means that the molten rock beneath the ocean floor keeps pumping minerals and other chemical nutrients into the oceans. In the past those materials have been washed onto the continents as the oceans have time and again flooded the land. Water from Earth's early hydrothermal vents may well have been the major source of all those mineral nutrients that early on served as a source for the buildup of those molecules of life that gave rise to the first living things on our planet. That idea is bound to be explored and tested by biologists who are dedicated to the study of the origin of life on Earth.

Life from the Stars?

When comet Hale-Bopp visited us in 1997, astronomers got a pretty good look at what the comet was made of. Biologists were especially interested to hear that the comet contained water, ammonia, formaldehyde, and hydrogen cyanide. Those chemicals can join to form amino acids, essential building blocks of living matter. We now can be certain that early in Earth's history many comets crashed into us and spread their matter far and wide. Not only could comets have supplied Earth with the basic "seeds," or molecules, essential to life, but their forceful impacts might well have triggered countless chemical reactions that led to the buildup of matter that became the first stirrings of life.

Astronomers who study those enormous clouds of gas and dust far out in space, called nebulae, have detected in the *nebulae* those same molecular seeds needed to build amino acids. And they have found actual amino acids in meteorites. Since Earth was formed out of one such nebula, there was no shortage of the complex molecules needed to get life started.

Panspermia

In the early 1900s, some scientists wondered if Earth life got its start somewhere else in the Universe and then somehow found its way here. That idea is called *panspermia* and was proposed in 1908 by the Swedish chemist Svante A. Arrhenius. Panspermia pictures bacteria being formed on some other planet beyond the

Comets, such as Hale-Bopp, contain water, ammonia, formaldehyde, and hydrogen cyanide. Those chemicals can join to form amino acids, essential building blocks of living matter. Not only could comets have supplied Earth with the basic "seeds," or molecules, essential to life, but their forceful impacts might well have triggered countless chemical reactions that led to the buildup of matter that became the first stirrings of life. Hale-Bopp's double tail is clearly visible in this photograph taken by Jim White from Trout Lake, Washington in March 1997.

Solar System. The bacteria then became attached to dust particles carried by wind, or in the debris blasted out of volcanoes, to the top of the atmosphere. Some escaped the planet's gravity and drifted through space until they were captured by Earth's gravity and so set up shop on Earth's surface or in its seas. Arrhenius imagined radiation from many stars blowing microscopic germs from one world to another.

As attractive as panspermia might be to some, it has two major problems. First, interstellar travel, even for bacteria, would be a dangerous voyage. And second, panspermia doesn't simplify the problem of the origin of life on Earth. It just shifts it to someplace else in the Universe. That thought explains the double-barreled question at the beginning of Chapter 1: *"How did life on planet Earth begin?"* But maybe we should rephrase the question to broaden our search for answers. Perhaps the question should be *"How may life arise, anywhere in the Universe?"* If we discovered life in a handful of alien dust from a planetary system remote from our own, we would still have to ask how that life got there. For those reasons, panspermia has lost the popularity it once enjoyed.

Life Elsewhere in the Solar System?

The search for life beyond Earth has been going on for many years, and at least one scientist—physicist Paul Davies—has not given up on panspermia. He was not surprised when some biologists thought they had spotted signs of primitive life in a meteorite. The meteorite was found in Antarctica in 1997. It is known, by its chemical composition, to have splashed off Mars a few billion years ago. Other scientists said no. Although the Mars meteorite debate has not been settled one way or the other, many scientists suspect that life probably did inhabit Mars in the distant past.

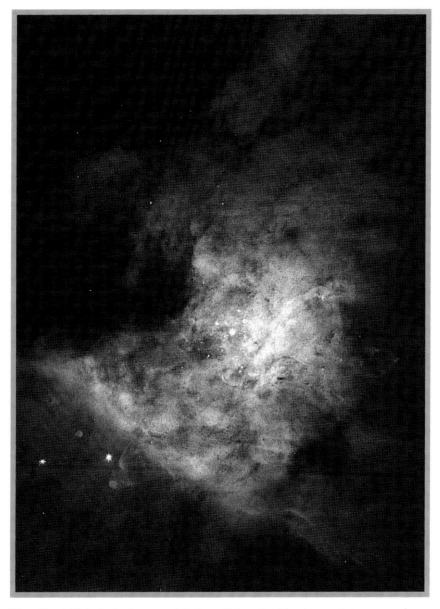

The Great Nebula in the constellation Orion the Hunter contains enough gas and dust to form upward of five thousand stars like the Sun. Among all that gas and dust are the same molecular "seeds" also found in comets and meteorites, chemical materials that can build amino acids. Since Earth was formed out of one such nebula, there was no shortage of the complex molecules needed to get life started.

Today Mars is a desert wasteland with a thin atmosphere mostly of carbon dioxide and virtually no oxygen. But long ago its volcanoes and active rock crust provided it with a dense atmosphere very different from the air it has today. And broad rivers carved out deep canyons. Conditions seem to have been just right to support life on Mars in its dim past. So far, however, the space probes sent to Mars to sample its sandy and rocky surface have failed to discover any traces of ancient life. But Davies and others hold that when future missions to Mars are able to dig deep down into its rocky crust, traces of once-living organisms are likely to be found. Davies has two interesting questions about those Martian life forms, if they are ever found: Did Mars life and Earth life arise independently? Or did Earth's early organisms get blasted off our planet by an asteroid impact and journey to Mars and start life there? Or could it have happened the other way around, which would make us transplanted Martians?

Until recently, conditions on the Solar System's other planets and their moons seemed far too harsh to support even the lowest life forms. But let's look at a possible exception—Jupiter's large moon Europa. In 1997 the Galileo space probe beamed back the sharpest photographs ever of Europa. It is completely covered over by ice floating on a planet-wide ocean of fresh water. Brown stains on the ice appear to be life-related chemicals, including hydrogen cyanide. According to NASA scientist Richard Terrile, "If this is indeed hydrogen cyanide, we have organic chemicals mixed into a bath of water. That's a recipe for life."

Planetary scientists now believe that Europa is geologically active. The crisscross of thousands of cracks in its blanket of ice may mean that the ocean water beneath is moving the ice around by itself being moved by heat welling up through the moon's rock floor. In short, some scientists suspect that Europa may have

The Arizona desert? No, a Martian landscape. Although no life forms have yet been detected on Mars by space probes that have landed on the red planet, some scientists hope one day to find primitive life forms deep within the Martian soil. If they do, then there will be many tantalizing questions: Will those life forms be similar to Earth's primitive life forms? How did life get started on Mars? Was it carried there from Earth or other regions of space? Or did it start independently from complex life-forming molecules brought by comets and meteorites billions of years ago?

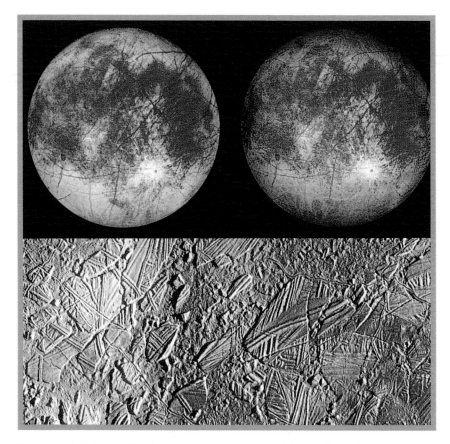

Europa, slightly smaller than our moon, is one of Jupiter's eighteen moons and a real puzzler. These images of Europa, made by the Galileo space probe, shows an icy surface resembling Earth's Arctic pack ice (detailed view at bottom). Scientists now think that a global ocean may slosh beneath the ice crust. One big question: Do life forms inhabit those dark ocean depths?

smokers that boil a rich chemical soup up through hydrothermal vents. Like the smokers being discovered in Earth's ocean floor, and possibly having given rise to microscopic organisms, the smokers of Europa might have done the same.

Are there other Solar System candidates for lowly life forms? The American astronomer Thomas Gold believes there may be

as many as ten—among them the Moon, Mars, three large asteroids, and two moons each of Jupiter and Saturn.

Life Beyond the Solar System?

Do we have evidence of life way out there in the Universe? No,
not yet. Will we ever? Maybe. As the British astronomer Sir
Martin Rees has said: "Absence of evidence is not the same as
evidence of absence."

Around 1996, astronomers began to find planets orbiting
stars far beyond the Sun. To date, about 20 have been found,
and that number probably will double over the next couple of
years. Right now our methods of studying those planets are so
poor that it's impossible to say much about their ability to support life. About all we know is that most of those planets are large
and rather too close to their stars. But that does not rule out
smaller—Earthlike—planets lying at safe distances from their
local star. After all, right now it's easier to find a big planet than
it is to find a smaller one.

Over the years astronomers have played a guessing game
of how many Earthlike planets that could support life are out
there. It has been an *exercise* in mathematics rather than an
exercise in observation, simply because we cannot see that far
very well. Without going through all the arithmetic, our best
guesses are that in the Milky Way galaxy alone there could be as
many as 10 million worlds with life forms of some sort. Suppose
for a moment that life arose on at least some of those Earthlike
planets. What we would want to know is what those life forms
are like. Did all of them follow the same or similar chemical path-
ways taken by early Earth life forms? For that to have happened,
each planet would have needed more or less the same chemical
soup that existed on early Earth. That seems very unlikely. Then

what might those other life forms be like? To some, that is the most exciting question we can ask about the Universe. But right now we don't have an answer.

Far beyond the Solar System and our home galaxy, countless billions more galaxies have planetary systems in numbers that would stagger the imagination. How many of those planetary systems support life is now impossible to say. One question we must ask is this: Since life arose on planet Earth, why shouldn't it also arise elsewhere in the Universe? This remarkable Hubble Space Telescope image shows two remote galaxies colliding.

Six

Gaia

Back to Earth

Gaia was the Greek goddess of Earth. The British chemist James Lovelock in 1974 adopted Gaia's name for his theory about a relationship he sees between the planet and its life forms. The two share a close biological union. Each affects the other's well-being in a living association called *symbiosis*. As Lovelock was developing his ideas, he was assisted by the American biologist Lynn Margulis.

Gaia theory says that Earth's living matter largely keeps the planet more or less the way it is, capable of supporting life. Despite ice ages that have piled up two-mile (3.2-kilometer)-thick layers of ice over large parts of the planet, and despite numerous peltings by comets and asteroids that have wiped out millions of species, the planet has remained habitable for nearly four billion years. Untold millions of species have come and gone, but the great chain of life has not been broken. Gaia is the union of three things: 1. All the living things that have ever existed, and all the ecosystems that have ever been; 2. Earth itself, with its oceans, atmosphere, and rocks; and 3. the Sun as a source of energy.

According to Lovelock, life actually controls and maintains conditions on the planet. It does so by responding to changes in climate and all other workings of the environment. It then regulates certain parts of the environment to best suit its needs. Recall that Earth's early atmosphere was very different from the air we breathe today. The oxygen revolution did not "just happen." It was brought on by living matter that learned how to carry out photosynthesis. While some of the planet's primitive organisms were poisoned by the massive buildup of atmospheric oxygen, others found it a better way to carry out life's many chemical reactions. Once the oxygen level reached about 21 percent of the total atmosphere, oxygen stopped accumulating and has remained just about the same ever since. Why? According to Gaia thinking, living organisms are maintaining that level. If the level increased only a few percent, the forests would burst into flame by spontaneous combustion. If it lowered only a few percent, there would be widespread death of many oxygen users.

Some scientists feel uncomfortable with the Gaia theory. They say that it's too fuzzy, that it can't be measured, too "unscientific." Others feel that it's at least an interesting way to view Earth, the only living planet we have yet found.

Any book about the origin of life must come back to the same haunting question: Since life happened here, why shouldn't it happen elsewhere? If life, intelligent life, is ever found on other worlds, what kind of biological garments will it wear? The American biologist Robert L. Sinsheimer has answered the question this way: "And so we look out to the stars for another sign of awareness. Do the stars look back? Is there on some distant planet a writer now describing his kind of life and proving that a life form such as ours could hardly be? Perhaps."

Among the thousands of deep sky images captured by the Hubble Space Telescope are many that show vast nebulous clouds of star matter in different stages of star formations. In this image of the nebula NGC 3603 we can see young bluish white giant stars only tens or hundreds of thousands of years old. Within the hydrogen cloud matter are older and less brilliant stars. There are also dense dark globs of gas and dust just now forming into stars. One cannot help but wonder if one or more such stars support intelligent life forms whose telescopic eyes are gazing in wonder at our own galaxy.

Glossary

Amino acids—complex molecules that were among the first molecules of life some four billion or so years ago. Amino acids contain carbon, oxygen, nitrogen, and hydrogen. These molecules are the building blocks of proteins. There are about 20 different kinds of amino acids.

Atom—the smallest possible piece of an element, consisting of protons, neutrons, and electrons. There are more than a hundred different kinds of atoms.

Biogenesis—the idea that only living things are able to produce other living things.

Coacervates—cell-like aggregates of molecules that the Russian scientist A. I. Oparin suggested may have been involved in the chemical evolution of the first living cells.

Cyanobacteria—among the earliest bacteria that learned to make their own food by combining hydrogen and carbon dioxide from the atmosphere. Cyanobacteria have survived from more than three billion years ago to the present.

Element—any substance made up of atoms, all of which have the same number of protons in the nucleus; for example, gold, sulfur, and oxygen are elements. An element cannot be broken down into, or built up from, a simpler substance by chemical means.

Gaia—the hypothesis that planet Earth and all of its living matter form a closed biological union, and that Earth's living forms regulate and maintain Earth conditions for their own well being.

Hydrothermal vents—geysers in the sea floor that pour out heat and numerous minerals that are capable of supporting a complex and diverse community of plants and animals. The vents also are called "smokers."

Microbe—the diverse microscopic organisms collectively called "germs."

Microsphere—microscopic sphere of proteinlike material that encloses itself within a membrane that separates it from the outside environment. Also called proteinoids, the tiny spheres were created in the laboratory by chemist Sydney Fox, a researcher into the origin of life on Earth.

Molecule—-the smallest piece of an element or a compound that continues to have the same chemical and physical properties.

Nebula—a vast cloud of hydrogen gas and molecular dust found in galaxies. Nebulae are regarded as the birthplaces of stars and planetary systems.

Nucleus—the control center of living cells.

Panspermia—the idea that bacteria reached Earth from other locations in the Universe and that Earth life was started by an invasion of such living matter rather than from the development of early life forms on Earth itself.

Photosynthesis—the action and ability of green plants to produce glucose by combining carbon dioxide and water vapor from the air in the presence of sunlight.

Planetesimals—chunks of rock, metals, and ices that were formed in the early life of the Solar System and that collected in ever-larger chunks that became the planets.

Protein—a complex molecule manufactured in cells and that serves the cell as a nutrient and as a building material.

Spontaneous generation—the discarded belief that living organisms, such as fleas, lice, fireflies, and even mice, could be created from such materials as fog, dew, or even dirty underwear mixed with wheat or corn.

Symbiogenesis—the idea that complex cells were built up by the union of two or more simpler cells or certain cell parts. The resulting new individual then inherited the different capabilities of each cell forming the union.

Further Reading

Allen, Tom. *The Quest*. Philadelphia: Chilton Books, 1965.

Beatty, J. Kelly. "Life At The Limit." *Sky & Telescope*, pp. 40–42, September 1999.

Bernstein, Max P., Scott A. Sandford, and Louis J. Allamandola, "Life's Far-Flung Raw Materials." *Scientific American*, pp. 42–49, July 1999.

Broad, William J. "Scientists Widen the Hunt for Alien Life." *The New York Times*, p. C1, May 6, 1997.

Calvin, Melvin. *Chemical Evolution*. Oxford: Oxford University Press. 1969.

Davies, Paul. *The Fifth Miracle*. New York: Simon & Schuster. 1999.

Delaney, John R. "Floor Show." *The Sciences*, pp. 27–33, July/August 1998.

Doolittle, W. Ford. "Uprooting the Tree of Life." *Scientific American*, pp. 90–95, February 2000.

Gallant, Roy A. *How Life Began*. New York: Four Winds Press, Scholastic, 1975.

———. *Before the Sun Dies: The Story of Evolution*. New York: Macmillan. 1989

———. *Beyond Earth: the Search for Extraterrestrial Life*. New York: Four Winds Press. Scholastic, 1977.

Goodrich, Norma Lorre. *The Ancient Myths*. New York: The New American Library, 1960.

Graves, Robert. *The Greek Myths*, 2 vols. London: Penguin Books, 1964.

Guerrero, Ricardo, and Lynn Margulis. "Stone Soup." *The Sciences*, pp. 34–38, July/August 1998.

Horgan, John. "In the Beginning . . ." *Scientific American*, pp. 116–125, February 1991.

Kormondy, Edward J. *Biology: A Systems Approach*. Menlo Park, CA: The Addison Wesley Publishing Co., 1988.

———. *General Biology, Vol. II: Organisms, Populations, and Ecosystems*. Dubuque, IA: William C. Brown Co., 1966.

Leach, Maria. *In The Beginning: Creation Myths Around the World*. New York: Funk & Wagnalls Company, 1956.

Lovelock, James. *The Ages of Gaia*. New York: W. W. Norton, 1988.

Malinowsky, Bronislaw. *Magic, Science, and Religion*. Garden City, NY: Doubleday & Company, Inc., 1954.

Margulis, Lynn. *Symbiotic Planet*. New York: Basic Books, 1998.

McSween, Harry Y., Jr. *Fanfare for Earth*. New York: St. Martin's Press. 1997.

Mercury. A special issue dedicated to Extraterrestrial Life. The Journal of the Astronomical Society of the Pacific, March-April 1999.

Middleton, John, ed. *Myth and Cosmos*. Garden City, NY: The Natural History Press, 1967.

Monastersky, R. "Signs of ancient life in deep, dark rock." *Science News*, p. 181, Sept. 20, 1997.

———. "The Rise of Life on Earth." *National Geographic*, pp. 54–81, March 1998.

Musser, George. "Here Come the Suns." *Scientific American*, p. 20, May 1999.

Ponnamperuma, Cyril. *The Origins of Life*. New York: E.P. Dutton, 1972.

Scientific American, special issue, "Revolutions in Science." (undated)

Simpson, Sarah. "Life's First Scalding Steps." *Science News*, pp. 24–26, January 9, 1999.

Thomas, Paul J. et al (Eds.). *Comets and the Origin and Evolution of Life*. New York: Springer 1997.

Wade, Nicholas. "Amateur Shakes Up Ideas on Recipe for Life." *The New York Times*, p. C1, April 22, 1997.

Young, Richard S. *Extraterrestrial Biology*. New York: Holt, Rinehart and Winston, Inc., 1966.

Index

Page numbers for illustrations are in **boldface**.